D1491721

A · COTTAGE FLORA

A · COTTAGE
FLORA

Illustrations by Peter Morter

Text by David MacFadyen

Foreword by Arthur Marshall

**SELECT
EDITIONS**

This edition published 1992 by the Promotional Reprint Company Limited, exclusively for Selecta Book Limited, Devizes, UK.

Illustrations Copyright © Peter Morter, Frank Phillips 1982
Text Copyright © David MacFadyen, Frank Phillips 1982

ISBN 1 85648 059 3

Printed and Bound in Malaysia

Contents

LATIN NAMES

Foreword

ARTHUR MARSHALL

Although many of us might envy the possessors of large and famous houses – Chatsworth, Blenheim, Petworth – for what such places usually contain in the way of pictures, furniture, books, silver and porcelain, one does not envy them their relative lack of flowers within sight of the house. At the best there is a distant display of formal box hedges laid out in a geometrical design and sometimes containing what appear to be, seen from afar, flowers. Many big houses have, and it's often quite a tramp to get there, a red-brick walled garden within it, again formally arranged, with flowers and fruit and vegetables: nothing really that ranks as 'a garden'.

The reason for the floral nudity of large houses is of course quite clear. A clump or two of arum lilies doing their best to cheer up the austere east front of Wentworth Woodhouse would merely look ludicrous. Beds of the humble nasturtium along the south of Hatfield House would seem to be an impertinence. *Brideshead Revisited* has acquainted us with the splendours of Castle Howard, splendours which at no point included flowers. By way of recompense, such houses do generally have rolling parkland, beautiful trees and distant views (sad how very quickly one tires of even the best views), but views, trees and parks are not flowers, and it is with the glory of flowers that we are here concerned.

The best gardens of all are what one calls in a general way 'cottage gardens', and their principal feature and charm is that not one inch of soil is without an occupant. And in many of them the flowers seem to be invading the house, so close do they press – lilies and hollyhocks (that underrated joy) rear themselves up to the windows, the wistaria hangs down and peers in, and two kinds of jasmine frame the sitting-room window. The Albertine rose brushes, in the slightest June breeze, the window panes, and repeats this affectionate gesture, if you're lucky, in October.

And in the nicest cottage gardens, sunflowers (another commonplace joy) rear their heads, and there are the spring glories of daffodil and snowdrop and crocus and, perhaps the best of all, the humble primrose (Primrose Day is April 19th and was my parents' wedding day). Later in the year who can resist the cornflowers, the forget-me-nots and the marigolds, clustering together behind, if you're lucky, a dwarf lavender border? And latest of all come the Michaelmas daisies and in the kind of colours worn by prim Victorian maiden ladies to church.

My love for such gardens began in childhood and at about the age of four. I was lucky enough to have grandparents with, and in Devon, what seemed to me at that age to be a sort of jungle of flowers, a magical place with red hot pokers towering high above my head and the lupins and irises just about level with my face. Grandparental indulgence allowed me to wander everywhere, and everywhere included games of hide-and-seek in and out of the flowers (I can recommend delphiniums as a good cover). At a lower level there were huge clumps of pinks (do I remember a pleasing variety called Her Majesty?), and masses of sweet-smelling stocks, and purple and yellow and light blue violas. There were asters and dahlias and geraniums, with everything growing together in a glorious profusion. Huge fuchsia hedges protected us from the winds, never very harsh in that blessed country, and here and there were hibiscus and vast hydrangeas, the latter kept miraculously blue by something that the gardener used to sprinkle round their roots (can it simply have been the contents of a blue bag?).

The hydrangeas flourished because there was something else that few gardens are fortunate enough to have – a Devon stream winding its way through, with two small islands in it, on which bamboos grew and provided shade from the sun. Here, while fat trout swam lazily about, I could imagine myself to be a member of Long John Silver's rascally crew, all going Yo-ho-ho and requiring rum.

There was a separate part of the garden reserved for roses. Say what you may, roses in a well-filled cottage garden never look quite right, struggling away for dear life with peonies and poppies and Canterbury bells. So a rose garden there was, out on its own and with what would nowadays, I suppose, be considered rather old-fashioned varieties – Merveille de Lyon (it was white), Margaret Dickson (a sort of pale flesh colour) and Caroline Testout (she was salmon pink). There was Maman Cochet, who was a salmony yellow and whom I always took to be the mother of the famous French tennis player of the twenties, and there was La France (silvery) and Ulrich Brunner (cherry red, with that German-sounding name too close to the First World War for comfort). And to climb up the walls of the house (it was a lofty Victorian building and needed all the covering it could get), what else could it have been in those far-off days but Gloire de Dijon (buff-coloured) and dear old Dorothy Perkins (pink and, I always disloyally thought, a bit insipid).

How astonished I would have been to know that the names of the flowers in which, in those wonderful summers when the sun always shone, or seemed to, I romped about all had meanings, often Greek or from the East, and the iris meant 'I have a message for you' ('tea's ready', I would doubtless have thought), and the double aster 'I share your sentiments', and the ranunculus 'I am dazzled by your charm'. Hard luck on the harebell (Grief) and the foxglove (Insincerity).

And now here are David MacFadyen and the superb illustrations of Peter Morter to instruct and delight pictorially all garden flower and herb lovers. How fascinating to learn that the beautiful delphinium or larkspur first sprang from the ground where Ajax's blood had fallen: that dill can not only cure hiccoughs (our Queen is said, at her christening, to have required an unusually large dose of dill-water) but was used by the Greeks as both a vegetable and an incense: that periwinkle was twined about the bodies of dead children and planted on their graves. Disappointing is the Scottish legend that the agreeable flower, sweet-william, was named after William Augustus, Duke of Cumberland, the dreaded 'Butcher' Cumberland of Culloden, and not sweet at all.

There is so much else. If honesty, whose white seed-pods are so highly prized by flower arrangers, grows well in a garden, it means that the owner is honesty itself. London pride owes its name, not to our capital city, but to the eighteenth-century firm of London & Wise.

In fact, treats and pleasures galore await you. Now read on . . .

Introduction

English cottage gardens grow out of English history, echoing in a subtle blending of decoration and usefulness the tastes, beliefs and ways of life of a hundred generations of countrymen.

The mediaeval peasant's garden was probably little more than a subsistence plot, in which he grew potherbs and the beans that he ground up to make flour. It was not until the Dissolution of the Monasteries in the 1530s that the first great enrichment came. Cut off from the herbal medicines supplied by the monks, villagers began to grow their own—agrimony, borage, comfrey, horehound, eyebright, pennyroyal, wormwood and many others—most no doubt lifted from the old monastery gardens together with a few Madonna lilies and white roses, long used in church decoration. Other herbs were grown to alleviate the monotony of salted or smoked meats, and still others for their sweet scent, like the lavender and rosemary that were mingled with rushes and strewn over the floors. Then too, there were the plants that were grown to make dyes—golden rod for yellow, for example, and flags for black.

All these brought colour to the garden, but all had a practical purpose, even the elder and peonies that were grown to ward off witchcraft and evil spirits, and the granny bonnet that was believed to keep plague away from the door. The cottager had little money to spend on luxuries, and obtained his plants as gifts, or by bartering cuttings with a neighbour; occasionally he would bring home some hedgerow novelty such as a clump of double primroses or albino bluebells. Vegetables, flowers and herbs shared the same beds in a charmingly ordered profusion that can still be seen in a few traditional gardens to this day. Beauty may have been incidental, but it was beauty nonetheless.

Perhaps the most popular time for importing

decorative plants into cottage gardens was the late eighteenth century, when the gentry, under the influence of Capability Brown, demolished acres of ornamental beds and replaced them with landscaped parks. Not sharing the same romantic attachment to wilderness, the cottagers seized upon the rejected plants and brought them triumphantly home. It is the descendants of many of these plants that are regarded as the old-fashioned cottage flowers of today.

Flowers have been man's companions for a very long time. They have attended, with their special meanings, his birth, marriage and death; they have cured his sickness (or have appeared to, which comes to the same thing); they have prophesied mirth or misery, protected him from evil, helped him in love and comforted him in despair; they have shown him beauty and taught him wonder; they have married legend and romance with reality.

Something of the story of this very special relationship is told in the pages of this book.

Anemone
:RANUNCULACEAE:

Native:	Height:	Flowers:	Duration:
Mediterranean	6–12 in.	February–April	about 6 weeks

The first anemone was created by the sorrowing Aphrodite from the blood of her beloved and expiring Adonis, thus ensuring that he would live for ever as a flower. Consequently, the plant has always been held sacred to Love; Roman lovers wove the flowers into chaplets. In the botany of Fairyland, however, it is considered that the crimson marks on the petals were painted there by fairy hands, and that the blossoms themselves offer shelter to elves in wet weather.

Other anemone lore is of less certain derivations. In England it was believed that the first spring-gathered anemone worn against the skin would keep the wearer safe from pestilence throughout the coming year. Other nations were not so sure, and held that, on the contrary, the scent of the flower was so noxious that to inhale it was to run the risk of severe illness. Traditionally, the Welsh would never plant anemones on graves because they are too sweet-smelling; but this was balanced by the Chinese, who always planted them on graves.

The plant's alternative name, 'windflower', comes from the Greek *anemos*, wind, and a legend, contradicting the Adonis story, says that the trembling flower was a virgin nymph beloved of Zephyr, god of the west wind. His jealous mistress, Flora, made the transformation in order to remove the temptation once and for all.

Angelica

:ANGELICA ARCHANGELICA:

Native:	Height:	Flowers:	Duration:
E. Mediterranean	6–10ft.	July–August	3–4 weeks

So numerous are the benefits that this generous herb has bestowed upon mankind that its virtues have been doubly extolled in its generic and specific names; not only angelic, but archangelic too.

Small boys have used its hollow stems as a means of blowing split peas or water at rivals; cooks candy the flower stems and the leaf-stalks and mid-ribs to make decorations for cakes and trifles, simmer the roots and leaves with rhubarb and apples to reduce acidity, or use them to make sweets and liqueurs. Modern herbalists recommend an infusion of the dried leaves as a soothing nerve-tonic, while the Lapps not only chew the stalks like tobacco, but crown their poets with garlands of the herb because its scent helps in summoning up the muse. In other parts of the world, angelica leaves are offered as a cure for smoking, or as a means of instantly dispelling the effects of alcohol.

The old-time herbalists were even more enthusiastic in their claims, vowing that angelica was 'contrarie to all poysons', including the bite of mad dogs and other venomous beasts. It was said, too, that to carry a piece of the root worn about the neck or in the pocket would render witches harmless and ward off elf-shots, the invisible but deadly arrows of the Little People. But the greatest demand for 'Root of the Holy Ghost' was in time of plague, as Du Bartas wrote:

> *Contagious aire ingendring pestilence*
> *Infects not those that in their mouths have ta'en*
> *Angelica, that happy counterbane*
> *Sent down from heav'n by some celestial scout*
> *As well the name and nature both avowt.*

Bluebell
:HYACINTHUS NON-SCRIPTUS:

Native:	Height:	Flowers:	Duration:
Europe	12in.	April–May	3–4 weeks

Everyone knows the name of the bluebell; but the flower that is beckoned to mind by the name depends very much on where you live. Scottish bluebells are called 'harebells' in England, while English bluebells are known as 'wild hyacinths' north of the Border. Therefore, the bluebell to which Sir Harry Lauder compared his Mary in *I love a lassie* was not the misty flower of the spring woods, but the robust, summer-blooming plant of the Scottish hills. It is a flower very dear to the Scottish heart; more dear, perhaps, than the Englishman's bluebell is to him:

> *Methinks in every hum of bee I hear,*
> *A breeze-born tinkling from my country's own bluebell*

—so runs an old Scots exile's lament. So Sir Harry would never have called Mary a 'wild hyacinth'; rhyming difficulties apart, this plant is also known in the north as 'auld-man's bells', a flower of ill omen if brought to an elderly person's house.

The English bluebell, which makes copses and West Country sea-meadows vibrate with colour in April and May, does not seem to have borne its present name for very long. The Elizabethans called it 'English jacinth' and, confusingly, 'hare-bell'. Gerard says that it grew 'every where thorow England' in his day, and mentions that 'the root is bulbous, full of a slimie, glewish juice, which will serve to set feathers upon arrowes in stead of glew, or to paste books with'. The same liquid, incidentally, made an excellent starch.

Borage
⸕ BORAGO OFFICINALIS ⸕

Native:	Height:	Flowers:	Duration:
Europe	2ft. plus	June–September	8–10 weeks

It seems that, after all, borage did not spring full-blown to life simply to grace tankards of alcoholic fruit cup clasped in the hands of débutantes at such tribal rites as Ascot and Henley. There is nothing new under the sun, and even in classical times it was noted that the leaves and flowers of borage put into wine made women and men glad and merry, driving away all sadness, dullness and melancholy and in general, promoting an exhilarating, lively air to the proceedings. Similar effects have been observed at many a May Ball, but perhaps few onlookers would be able to confirm, with Gerard, that the herb 'comforteth the heart ... and quieteth the phrentike or lunaticke person'.

All the same, it is most accommodating. Its vivid blue flowers will enliven a dull corner of the garden for weeks on end, and can then be crystallized to enhance iced birthday cakes. It seeds itself easily—some gardeners think too easily—giving an almost endless supply of young leaves which can be finely chopped and added, with whole flowers, to salads. It adds a cool, cucumber flavour to soups, and its leaves, infused to make a tea, provide a delightfully refreshing tonic, especially when lemon and sugar are added.

And, of course, no garden party or chilled summer punch is complete without the charm and tang of borage—the first supplied by the flowers, the second by the leaves.

Canterbury bells

——:CAMPANULA MEDIUM:——

Native:	Height:	Flowers:	Duration:
Europe	1½–3ft.	May–July	3–4 weeks

Probably the most evocative hymn to the awakening of the English spring is the opening to the *Prologue* of *The Canterbury Tales*:

Whenne that April with his showres sote
The Drought of March hath pierced to the rote,
And bathed every vein in such licour,
Of which virtue engendered is the flower . . .

Then, said Chaucer, was the time that folk longed to go on pilgrimages, and especially to the shrine of St Thomas à Becket at Canterbury, 'the holy blissful Martyr for to seek'. He conjures up the Knight, the Nun, the Pardoner, the Miller and the rest, all riding south-east, doubtless jingling the little bells it was customary for pilgrims' horses to wear on their harness. And it was from these bells that the blue flowers which grew so plentifully in the Kentish woods were named.

Some authorities disagree, however, and say that the flower was so named long before the pilgrimages to Becket's tomb began, and was sacred to St Augustine, though no one seems to know why. Augustine began his conversion of the English at Thanet in AD 597, and, having made a Christian of King Ethelbert of Kent, was granted the see of Canterbury as Archbishop of the English. Perhaps Canterbury bells were plentiful in Kent in his day too, and he simply liked them. But by Chaucer's time he was chiefly remembered for having cursed the people of Rochester for throwing fish heads at him. He swore that henceforth all children born in Rochester would have tails, and for centuries it was fervently believed that all its citizens were so decorated.

Comfrey

——:SYMPHYTUM OFFICINALE:——

Native:	Height:	Flowers:	Duration:
Europe	to 3ft.	throughout summer	3–4 months

Comfrey has many different names: knitbone, ass-ear, boneset, consound, consolida. Most of these give clues to its many medicinal or culinary uses, and bear witness to the fact that no well-stocked herb garden would have been considered complete without it. There seems to have been no end to its usefulness. Baker, in his *Jewell of Health* published in 1567, says that 'the water of the greater Comferie drunke helpeth such as are bursten, and that haue broken the bone of the legge'; the hairy leaves applied as a poultice would accelerate the healing of any ulcer or wound; and if a decoction of the leaves were taken internally, it would aid a speedy recovery from most internal maladies, including consumption. 'Consound' means 'against swooning', and refers to the old practice of administering an infusion of comfrey to those subject to the vapours. There is also a rather curious early nineteenth-century remedy for whooping-cough and consumption, which suggests mingling juice of comfrey with West Indian brown sugar and boiling them together into a kind of toffee.

The old name 'consolida' tells of the plant's ability to bind or glue together, and for this reason the roots were used in cooking since, if they were boiled with odd fragments of meat, they would unite them in a single and more appetizing mass. However, it is more usual nowadays to chop the young leaves into a salad, or to cook them as spinach topped with white sauce and grated cheese.

Even in death the plant has one last favour to grant. Throw it on the compost heap; it speeds the breakdown of all the other materials into good mulch.

Cornflower

⋮CENTAUREA CYANUS⋮

Native:	Height:	Flowers:	Duration:
Europe	1–3ft.	June–September	7–8 weeks

The first part of the generic name of this plant is said to be derived from Chiron, the centaur. It was he who taught men the use of medicinal herbs, and was especially grateful to this one because it cured him of a wound inflicted by an arrow envenomed with the blood of the Hydra. The cornflower has been accredited with the ability to drive away snakes ever since.

The second part is derived from the youth Cyanus, who so loved the vivid blue flowers that he spent all his time in the cornfields making garlands of them, and always wore garments of the same hue. This so touched the goddess Flora that when he died, surrounded by the flowers he had picked, she transformed his body into the plant.

None of this impressed Gerard very much, for he gives the flower the old English countryman's name of 'hurt-sicle', 'because it hindreth and annoyeth the reapers by dulling and turning the edges of their sicles in reaping of corne'. However, since it is 'of temperature something cold', it may be efficacious against inflammation of the eyes. Even to this, he doubtfully adds the words, 'as some thinke'.

CENTAUREA CYANUS

CENTAUREA MONTANA

Crocus

Native:	Height:	Flowers:	Duration:
Asia Minor	4in.	October	2–3 weeks

In odd patches of undisturbed land, such as old churchyards, on the Cambridgeshire/Essex border, you sometimes see the purple heads of saffron crocus peering through the fading autumn grass. Some local people aver that these are the descendants of the millions that used to be grown hereabouts to make saffron dye; it is hard to believe it, since the industry perished two hundred years ago, but if it is not the case, where do they come from?

Saffron Walden was the centre of the trade, and old writers tell of the country round about, in October, 'looking merrily with most lovely saffron'. The flowers were picked in that month, and the yellow dye was produced from their stigmas. Apparently it took 4,320 flowers to make one ounce of saffron; nevertheless, the crop was a profitable one since the product was in demand not only for dyeing, but also for flavouring cakes and for use in medicines. Marigold flowers, nutmeg and saffron make a most cheering cordial.

The medicinal and supposed amatory virtues of the saffron crocus have been known for thousands of years. The ancient Greeks strewed bridal beds with them, perhaps because it was one of the flowers that made up the bed of Zeus and Hera, and Solomon sang, 'Thy plants are an orchard of pomegranates ... camphire and spikenard; spikenard and saffron'.

It seems a pity that no longer do 'the Cantabrian hills the purple saffron show': sugar beet is not nearly so attractive.

Crown imperial
——:FRITILLARIA IMPERIALIS:——

Native:	Height:	Flowers:	Duration:
Himalayas	2–3 ft.	April	3–4 weeks

This delightful flower, which seems so jauntily foreign in our gardens, has actually been with us for hundreds of years. Gerard says it was common in London gardens even in his day, at the end of the sixteenth century, and goes on to give a loving description of it. He comments upon the strange, foxy odour of the bulbs, of which any gardener who has ever put a spade through one is aware, and tells of the bells, at the bottom of each of which 'there is placed six drops of most cleare shining sweet water, in taste like sugar, resembling in shew faire orient pearles; the which drops if you take away, there immediately appeare the like'.

One story of the plant's origin says that once it was a beautiful and virtuous queen:

A Queen she was whom ill report belied,
And a rash husband's jealousy destroyed;
Driv'n from his bed and court the fields she ranged,
Till spent with grief was to a blossom changed,
Yet only changed as to her human frame;
She kept th' Imperial beauty and the name.

Another story recounts that long ago the crown imperial grew tall, straight and white, and stood so even through the agony of Jesus in the Garden of Gethsemane, when all the other flowers bowed their heads to the ground. But when the soldiers came to take Him away, He looked at the crown imperial which, overwhelmed by remorse, drooped its head and blushed for shame, while tears of contrition filled its cups. And thus it has stood ever since.

Daffodil

═:NARCISSUS:═

Native:	Height:	Flowers:	Duration:
Europe	12in.	April	3–4 weeks

Long before they flashed upon Wordsworth's inward eye, daffodils, or narcissi, had been a boon to poets, chiefly for the prettily fanciful tales told of their origins. It is generally held to be the white variety that sprang from the body of the Greek youth Narcissus as he lay by a brook-side, transfixed by the reflection of his own loveliness, though Addison says that when the nymphs came to look for him, they only found 'A rising stalk with yellow blossoms crown'd'. It seems certain, however, that the cup in the flower's centre of all varieties contains the tears of Narcissus.

Another legend tells how Earth first put forth the flowers to lure the lovely Proserpine for Pluto, god of the underworld. The daffodil's beauty caused the maid's attention to waver for a moment, enabling Pluto to rush from his lair and seize her. It was with some justice, therefore, that the ancients labelled the narcissus the flower of deceit, and because it was also the last bloom she plucked, the flower of imminent death.

Delphinium

——:(LARKSPUR) DELPHINIUM AJACIS:——

Native:	Height:	Flowers:	Duration:
Mediterranean	1–3ft.	June–August	4–5 weeks

Childhood would be diminished without A. A. Milne's dormouse who lived in a flower-bed because,

Wherever he looked, he'd a wonderful view
Of geraniums (pink) and delphiniums (blue),

though from the slight evidence available, it seems that the delphiniums that so enchanted the creature were likely to have been the tall, stately, showy varieties, rather than the delicate larkspur.

Yet the larkspur has the nobler antecedents, for, as its specific name bears witness, it was born of the blood of Ajax, who, excepting only Achilles, was the greatest of all the Greek warriors before the walls of Troy. The story is that, after the death of Achilles, both Ajax and Odysseus laid claim to the arms and armour of the dead hero, and after some debate Atreus, on behalf of the Greeks, awarded them to Odysseus as being the wiser of the two. Ajax was so piqued by this that, blinded with rage, he attacked and slew a flock of sheep, believing them to be the sons of Atreus. As his anger cooled, he saw his error. Bitterly ashamed, he turned his sword— the one presented to him by Hector, war-captain of the Trojans—upon himself. Where his blood spurted upon the ground, the larkspur grew. The petals are said to bear the letters AI, being both the sigh that Earth emitted on receiving Ajax's blood, and the first two letters of his name.

It was believed, too, that if larkspur were thrown at a snake, it would paralyse it, and render it unable to strike until the flower was removed.

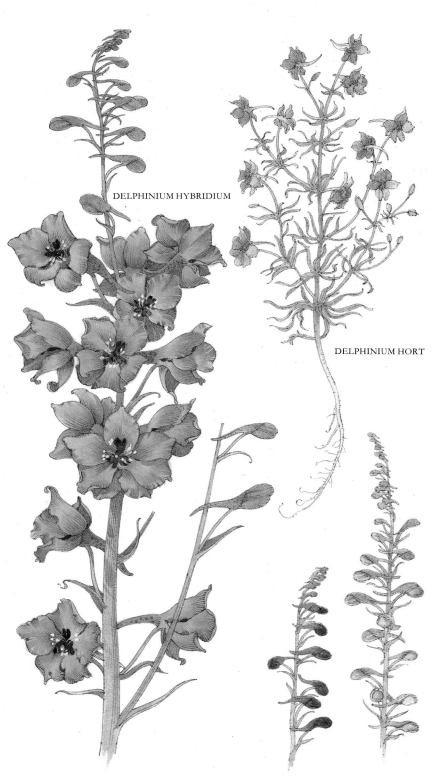

DELPHINIUM HYBRIDIUM

DELPHINIUM HORT

Dill

—:PEUCEDANUM GRAVEOLENS:——

Native:	Height:	Flowers:	Duration:
Europe	3ft.	June–August	4–6 weeks

The name comes from the old Saxon *dille*, to lull or soothe, and for centuries the seeds boiled in water or wine were taken as a tranquillizer; the word still occurs in its old sense in some northern dialects—to dill (calm) a toothache, or to dill (lull) a child to sleep. Nicholas Culpeper in his *British Herbal* says that 'Dill, being boiled and drunk, is good to ease swellings and pains; it also stayeth the belly and stomach from casting . . . it stayeth the hiccough', all of which are good reasons why some old-fashioned mothers still give their infants dill-water to ease the gripe.

The Greeks used dill as a vegetable and as incense in their temples, and in the early Middle Ages it was considered efficacious against both 'water-elf disease', which, from the symptoms described, seems to have been chicken-pox, and jaundice. It was also much used by witches as one of the less repellent ingredients in their potions; however, it could be turned against them too. According to Michael Drayton:

> . . . *her Vervayne and her Dill*
> . . . *hindreth Witches of their Will.*

Though it can seldom be used for this purpose nowadays, dill is still regarded as an essential plant in any well-stocked herb garden. Chopped dill leaves make an excellent sauce for fish or, mixed with cottage cheese, a superb sandwich filling. The anise flavour is stronger in the seeds, and these can be used to flavour lamb stews or to make a herb vinegar for pickling gherkins. It is not a good idea to plant dill and fennel side by side. Their similarity can lead to some awkward culinary confusion.

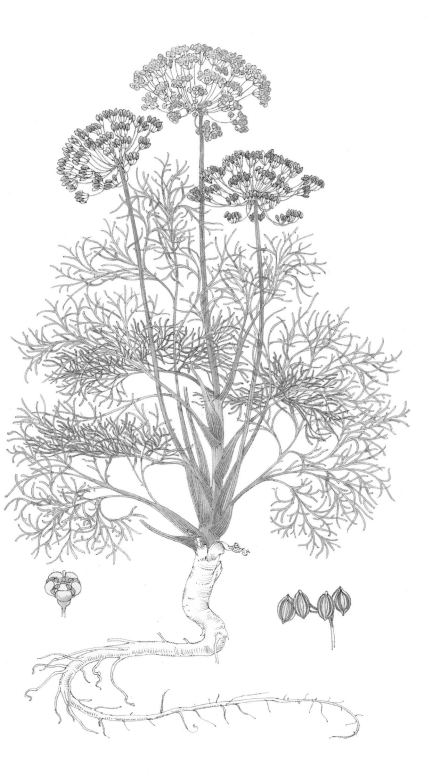

Eglantine

⸱(SWEETBRIAR) ROSA RUBIGINOSA⸱

Native:	Height:	Flowers:	Duration:
Europe	8ft.	June	2-3 weeks

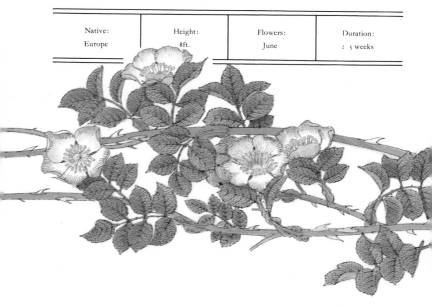

It is apt that eglantine should flower in June, that loveliest of months in England, for its sweet fragrance is the very essence of the short, balmy nights and hushed, expectant dawns. Shakespeare must have been aware of this when, in *A Midsummer Night's Dream*, he included it among his list of plants for the 'bank whereon the wild thyme blows'. Shelley too envisaged it as one of the plants that made up the distillation of summer:

> *And in the warm hedge grew lush eglantine,*
> *Green cowbind and the moonlight-coloured may . . .,*

and Rupert Brooke, in exile from his beloved Grantchester, and among the disciplined tulips of Berlin remembered wistfully how 'unkempt about those hedges blows, an English unofficial rose'.

Fennel

Native:	Height:	Flowers:	Duration:
Europe	5–8ft.	July–August	2–3 weeks

The green, misty leaves and the tiny, yellow, umbelliferous flowers of fennel have graced country gardens for centuries, and the virtues of the plant have been celebrated almost since time's beginning. Generally, the accent has been upon its strengthening qualities; gladiators used to eat it before entering the arena; victorious Greek warriors were decked with it—'He who battled and subdued, a wreath of fennel wore'—while in England, farmers mixed it with soap and salt and pressed it into a hole at the head of the plough to strengthen the land and improve its yield. The strengthening aspect was also the theme in mind when it was strewn across the path of newly married couples; and it was this association with weddings that made poor Ophelia include fennel in her tragic bouquet.

Both leaves and seeds, with their anise flavour, are an invaluable adjunct to cookery, especially if used with fish, cheese dishes, soups and pickles. Fennel tea has been regarded as a slimming agent since Roman times, and as an aid to digestion. It is one of the ingredients of gripe-water, and it was imbibed, in a mixture of other things, by Louis XIV, as a palliative for pangs caused by over-eating.

Gerard says that 'the pouder of the seed of Fennell drunke for certaine daies together fasting preserveth the eyesight', and quotes:

Of Fennell, Roses, Vervain, Rue and Celandine,
Is made a water good to cleere the sight of eine.

Forget-me-not
ːMYOSOTISː

Native:	Height:	Flowers:	Duration:
temperate Europe, Asia	6–12 in.	April–May	about 2 months

Though the name has been applied to a wide number of plants down the ages, since the sixteenth century at least, forget-me-not has signified to the English the pale, misty blue flowers that drift like a cloud over every garden in the late spring. They declare true love and—as every gardener knows who has ever tried to get rid of them—constancy. The plants should be exchanged by friends each leap year on 29 February, or presented to anyone making a journey on that day.

One or two species have curved racemes resembling a scorpion's tail; this gave rise to the alternative name of 'scorpion grass', and to the idea that the plant could cure the stings of both scorpions and serpents. In Siberia, where such creatures are rare, it was considered efficacious in the treatment of venereal disease.

Above all, however, the flower symbolizes remembrance, and it is said that for years after 1815 it was banked in shoals on the battlefield of Waterloo; it is also believed that if you plant it on the grave of someone you love, it will never die as long as you live. One version of the origin of its most popular name comes from an old German legend in which a knight and his lady, strolling by the Danube, spied a clump of the flowers drifting by. Forgetting the weight of his armour, the knight hurled himself into the stream to obtain them for her:

> *And the lady fair of the knight so true,*
> *Aye remembered his hapless lot:*
> *And she cherished the flower of brilliant hue,*
> *And braided her hair with the blossoms blue.*
> *And she called it 'Forget-me-not'.*

Foxglove

⫶DIGITALIS PURPUREA⫶

Native:	Height:	Flowers:	Duration:
W. Europe	3ft.	June–July	6 weeks

'Witches' gloves', 'deadmen's bells', 'bloody fingers'—all the alternative names for the foxglove have a sinister ring about them. Perhaps they came about because, when the long stalk bends over, it is supposed to indicate the presence of a supernatural being; but the names are more likely to be due to the plant's long association with the Black Arts. It was one of the ingredients of an ointment which, when rubbed on their thighs, enabled witches to fly; apart from baby fat and the like, the more effective contents of the concoction were foxglove (digitalis, a heart stimulant), deadly nightshade (belladonna, a hallucinatory drug) and hemlock, which induces unconsciousness. So no doubt an application of the ointment did produce some result.

On a more cheerful note, country people have long known that the storage qualities of potatoes, tomatoes and apples are much improved if foxgloves are grown nearby, and that cut flowers will last longer in water if foxgloves are included in the arrangement. If they are unsuitable, then add foxglove tea to the water in the vase—the brew is made by pouring boiling water over a handful of leaves and flowers and leaving them to steep overnight. Centuries ago, the poor used to drink the tea as an intoxicant, but this is highly inadvisable; digitalis can kill.

Garlic

⁚ALLIUM SATIVUM⁚

Native:	Height:	Flowers:	Duration:
Central Asia	1–3ft.	June	2–3 weeks

Garlic was the food of heroes, or at least of such heroes as the labourers on the pyramids and the centurions and legionaries of the Roman army. But, as a rule, it did not greatly appeal to the upper classes. Egyptian priests were forbidden to eat it before attendance at the temple, and Horace tells of a sleepless night resulting from eating garlic at the house of a friend. After wonderingly commenting upon the strength of the stomachs of farm-workers who consumed it as part of their regular diet, he moans, 'What is this venom savaging my frame? Has viper's blood, unknown to me, been brewed into these herbs?' The aroma too, was considered indelicate; in *A Midsummer Night's Dream*, when the clowns are going to play before the court, they are advised to eat no onions or garlic, 'for we are to have sweet breath'.

However, even in ancient times, the herb was valued as an antiseptic and a sure defence against cholera and typhus; as recently as the First World War, the French army used garlic to cleanse wounds, in the same way as the British used iodine. As every student of Hammer Films knows, it also provides one of the few certain means of warding off the forces of the supernatural. Cloves of garlic were buried at crossroads to confound Hecate, goddess of the witches; werewolves and witches were powerless against anyone carrying a piece of the herb, and garlands of it were hung on cottage doors when it was suspected that witches were abroad.

Gerard says that if you have a mole in the garden, you should place garlic in his run, 'and you shall see him run out, astonied'; and another gardening tip is to put garlic into the rose-bed—greenfly cannot endure it.

Geranium

——:(CRANESBILL) GERANIUM PRATENSE:——

Native:	Height:	Flowers:	Duration:
N. Europe	18–30in.	July–September	2 months

Meadow cranesbill, dove's-foot, the true English geranium, is of a blue so pure and tender that it seems positively to sing. In many old gardens it announces the full triumph of summer and is quite often seen, in mixed borders, in the company of rosebay willowherb, the pink and the blue complementing each other to perfection.

But it is not the loveliness of the plant that captivates Gerard, in his *Herball* of 1597, so much as its qualities as a panacea for all kinds of bodily ills. 'The herbe and roots dried', he says, 'and beaten into most fine pouder, and given half a spoonful fasting, and the like quantitie to bedwards in red wine or old claret for the space of one and twenty daies together, cure miraculously ruptures or burstings, as my selfe have often proved, whereby I have gotten crownes and credit'. If the patient is elderly, however, the recipe should be varied slightly. You should then 'adde thereto the powder of red snails (those without shels), dried in an oven in number nine, which fortifieth the herbes in such sort, that it never faileth, although the rupture be great and of long continuance ... as my selfe have likewise proved'— though whether upon himself or a patient he does not make clear.

The name of the plant, incidentally, is derived from the fruit's fancied resemblance to the head and bill of a crane; or to a dove's foot, which gives it its older name.

Golden rod

⸝SOLIDAGO VIRGAUREA⸝

Native: Europe, N. America	Height: 3–6ft.	Flowers: August–October	Duration: 4–5 weeks

This glowing plant, so often the last bright player on summer's stage, was for centuries thought to indicate the presence of fairy gold, or other buried treasure, in the soil beneath, and if it should spring up beside a cottage without being planted by the householder, then good fortune would certainly follow. It took a great deal of disillusionment to dispel these notions, it seems, for they were still believed in many country districts in Queen Victoria's day.

In the hands of a dowser, golden rod is said to be as effective as hazel for detecting hidden springs; but its chief use was as a stauncher of blood from wounds, and it was greatly valued as such. In the early years of Queen Elizabeth's reign, it was imported in a dried state and sold in the London streets at half a crown an ounce, but the bottom dropped out of the market when it was found growing wild in Hampstead. Gerard's sturdy common sense emerges when he comments that now 'no man will give half a crowne for a hundredweight of it, which plainly setteth foorth our inconstancie and sudden mutabilitie, esteeming no longer of anything how pretious soever it be than while it is strange and rare. This verifieth our English Proverbe "Far-fecht and deere-bought is best for Ladies". Yet it may be more truly said of fantasticall physitions that when they have found ... a perfect remedy neere home ... they will seeke for another farther off, and by that means many times hurt more than they helpe.'

Honesty

——:LUNARIA ANNUA:——

Native:	Height:	Flowers:	Duration:
Europe	about 2½ft.	May–June	4–6 weeks

Gerard, in his *Herball* of 1597, says that in his day honesty used to grow wild 'about Pinner and Harrow on the Hill, and Essex likewise about Horn-church'. It is doubtful if it does so any more, though it is still widely cultivated for its large, white seed-pods, 'thinne and clear shining, like a shred of white Sattin newly cut from the peece', which make the plant so useful in dried flower arrangements. It is these bright discs, too, that give honesty its alternative names of 'lunary' and 'moonwort', and, via the Doctrine of Signatures (which holds that cures may be effected by plants bearing some resemblance to the affected part or its ailment), promoted the idea that they were efficacious in treating cases of lunacy. But this was a complex business, according to the Elizabethan poet Michael Drayton who, in describing one such experiment, says:

> *Then sprinkles she the juice of Rue*
> *With nine drops of the midnight dew,*
> *From Lunarie distilling.*

It has long been thought that wherever honesty grows well, the householder is exceptionally honest, but no one seems to know why. Could it be because the transparent pods hold the seeds with the minimum of concealment?

Honeysuckle

:LONICERA PERICLYMENUM:

Native:	Height:	Flowers:	Duration:
Europe, W. Asia	to 20ft.	July–August	3–4 weeks

There was a popular song at the turn of the century, whose refrain was, 'You are my honey, honeysuckle, I am the bee'. This was just one of a long line of ballads, stories and poems that associate the plant with lovers, either for the magnetism of its sweetly scented flowers or for the clinging habit of its growth. Both are celebrated equally, whether it is called by its present name or by its older one of 'woodbine'. In *A Midsummer Night's Dream*, Titania tells Bottom that she will wind him in her arms as 'doth the woodbine, the sweet honeysuckle gently entwist'. Much earlier, Chaucer envisaged honeysuckle as a symbol of constancy, believing that those who wore chaplets on their heads

> *Of fresh Wodebind be such as never were*
> *To love untrue in word, ne thought, ne dede,*
> *But ay stedfast . . .*

Sweethearts exchanged posies of the flowers in the same spirit, and sometimes the plants were grown upon graves as a mark of eternal fidelity.

The Elizabethans valued honeysuckle, both as a liniment 'to annoint the body that is benummed', and as an aid in constructing the covered walks, bowers and 'pleasaunces' that made gardens of the period a paradise for lovers and eavesdroppers. Thus, in *Much Ado about Nothing*, Beatrice learns of Benedick's love by overhearing Hero's conversation from a bower where 'honeysuckles, ripen'd by the sun, forbid the sun to enter'.

Iris

─────:(YELLOW FLAG) IRIS PSEUDACORUS:─────

Native:	Height:	Flowers:	Duration:
Europe	2–4ft.	May–August	4–6 weeks

This superb golden flower flourishes best in the damper parts of the garden, by a slow-moving stream, perhaps, or a pond, where it stands complacently just out of reach, attended by guardian dragonflies flashing iridescent blue.

The three leaves of the flower are said to symbolize faith, wisdom and courage, and it was for these virtues that the old Frankish kings carried a flag in bloom when they were proclaimed. Later, in 1137, Louis VII adopted a stylized version as a device for his banner when he set off on the Second Crusade, and the flower became known as *fleur-de-Louis*, which was quickly corrupted into *fleur-de-luce*, or *fleur-de-lys*. The English came to know it well as 'flower-de-luce', especially after Edward III quartered his own arms with the device when he laid claim to the French crown some two hundred years later. And, despite Shakespeare's doleful prophecy in *Henry VI, Part I*,

Cropp'd are the flower-de-luces in your arms:
Of England's coat one half is cut away,

it remained on the British royal escutcheon until the beginning of the nineteenth century. It was therefore somewhat tactless of Henry V, when he wooed Princess Katharine of France in his fractured French, to address her as his 'fair flower-de-luce'.

Lavender

——: LAVANDULA SPICA :——

Native:	Height:	Flowers:	Duration:
Mediterranean	3ft.	July–September	3–4 weeks

In the fields about Heacham in Norfolk, towards the end of July or the beginning of August, there is harvested the loveliest of crops—great billowing waves of blue-purple lavender that perfume the air for miles around—whose essence is distilled to create the most English of scents: lavender water.

Once, it is said, the lavender possessed no scent, until a day when the Virgin spread the Holy Child's swaddling clothes upon a lavender bush to dry; since then, the plant 'breathes of Paradise'. True or not, to most of us it breathes at least of nostalgia; of great bowls of pot-pourri in gleaming-floored country houses; of bees booming drowsily in lavender bushes at the edge of a herb garden; of nights spent, like Keats's heroine in *St Agnes' Eve*, beneath 'blanch'd linen, smooth and lavender'd'.

It is thought that the name of the plant comes from the Latin *lavare*, to wash, since the Romans used to bathe in lavender-scented water. They found it refreshing, and it was in this role that the herb was to be valued for many centuries to come. Before the popularizing of eau-de-Cologne, a dab of lavender water on the temples was considered ideal treatment for the vapours; drunk with ground nutmeg, cinnamon and cloves, it was thought an excellent remedy against the 'panting and passion of the heart'. Of less certain benefit, however, was Edward Lear's suggestion in *The Pobble who has no toes*:

> *His Aunt Jobiska made him drink*
> *Lavender water tinged with pink,*
> *For she said, 'The world in general knows*
> *There's nothing so good for a Pobble's toes!'*

Lily of the valley
CONVALLARIA MAJALIS

Native:	Height:	Flowers:	Duration:
N. Hemisphere	6–8in.	April–May	1 month

L**ong ago, perhaps in the sixth century, there lived in St Leonard's Forest in Sussex a fearsome dragon,** whose fiery breath and dreadful fangs were the terror of the neighbourhood. Fortunately, the country people had a champion in St Leonard, who also dwelt in the forest and, over the years, fought many a battle with the creature before finally overcoming it, to the relief of the peasantry. God also approved, for He decreed that henceforward no adder should bite in the forest, nor nightingale sing, since the bird had disturbed the hermit-saint's prayers, and that wherever the good man's blood had been spilt during the fighting, there lilies of the valley would grow. And so they do, to this day.

The flowers also grow wild in several other places in England, as well as being cultivated in gardens, originally for their sweet, powerful scent which was considered to be an excellent remedy for nervous complaints. Water distilled from the plant was much valued as a specific against a large number of disorders, ranging from headache, constipation and apoplexy, to dropsy and gout, but it is hard to see why. Lilies of the valley contain glucosides, which cause fluttering of the heart, like digitalis.

Only in Devon did people have their doubts; there it was thought that anyone who planted a bed of the flowers would be dead within a year.

London pride

—:SAXIFRAGA × UBIRCUM:——

Native:	Height:	Flowers:	Duration:
UK (hybrid)	12in.	May	3–4 weeks

Noël Coward seldom made any display of botanical knowledge. One of the few occasions on which he did so was in his famous wartime lyric:

London Pride has been handed down to us,
London Pride is a flower that's green:
London Pride means our own dear town to us ...

That is, he saw the plant as the age-old symbol of the indomitable spirit of the city he loved; as personifying, in its toughness and endurance, the London that showed:

Every blitz your resistance toughening
From the Ritz to the Anchor and Crown ...

Sadly, though, he was a little amiss. In fact, London pride is a hybrid created by a Mr London, of the gardening firm of London & Wise, in the eighteenth century. But it is a small point; and Mr Coward's heart was, as always, in the right place.

Since London pride was born in the Age of Reason, few legends are attached to the plant itself, but its ancestors and relations are the saxifrages that grow in cracks in rock. Long ago, it was noticed that, after growing awhile, the plants can split a rock apart, and because of this were used in the treatment of kidney- and gall-stones.

Perhaps Mr Coward's symbolism is the happier image.

Lungwort

:PULMONARIA OFFICINALIS:

Native:	Height:	Flowers:	Duration:
Central Europe	12in.	April–May	3–4 weeks

The Doctrine of Signatures is an ancient and rather charming belief that God, in response to the maladies wished upon us by the Devil, has provided antidotes on our hillsides, and in our woodlands and meadows. Each of these remedies, or rather, the herbs from which they are derived, is stamped with a characteristic, or Signature, that tells us how to use it. The characteristic may be in the colour of the plant, or in its shape, or in the form of its flowers or fruit. Whatever it is, it is fancied to bear some resemblance to a disease, or its cause, or a part of the body, and the plant was therefore considered the ideal agent for effecting a cure.

In the case of lungwort, the white spots on the green leaves were thought to resemble tubercular scars, and the plant was much sought after in consequence as a specific against consumption. How effective it was is hard to say, but at least there is no record of its having done anyone any harm. Curiously enough, it is still recommended by some modern herbalists as an aid for coughs, sore throats and hoarseness. The recipe is to boil two tablespoonfuls of crushed leaves in a cupful of water; the dosage is one cup per day. The plant is also known as 'Jerusalem cowslip', and 'Jerusalem sage', but its connection with Jerusalem is obscure.

Lupin

⸺⁚LUPINUS POLYPHYLLUS⁚⸺

Native:	Height:	Flowers:	Duration:
S. Europe, W. America	3–5 ft.	May–June	2–3 weeks

Great banks and shoals of peppery-scented lupins seem almost as essential to the calendar image of the cottage garden as a small child in a pinafore. Yet most of the varieties we see originated in about 1826 in the United States, when a Mr George Russell crossed *L. Polyphyllus* with *L. arboreus*, or bush lupins. However, in southern Mediterranean countries, the seeds have been considered excellent fodder for beast and man since ancient times. Pliny, for example, was of the opinion that few foods are more wholesome than white lupins, which, if eaten regularly, give one a good colour and a cheerful countenance. Mediaeval Englishmen took this notion to a further stage and praised the lupin for its aphrodisiacal qualities; ever-hopeful, perhaps, the English ascribed this virtue to each new plant that came their way, from potatoes to tomatoes.

In parts of Italy there is a strange legend that lupins were cursed by the Virgin Mary because, during the Flight into Egypt the flower betrayed the Holy Family's presence to Herod's soldiers by the rattling of its seed-pods.

There is an old saying too, that the plant's name comes from the Latin *lupus*, wolf, because it was believed to destroy the fertility of the soil in which it grew.

64

Marguerite

⸺:BELLIS PERENNIS:⸺

Native:	Height:	Flowers:	Duration:
Europe	to 4in.	March–October	throughout summer

The French name for a daisy is *marguerite*, the same as that for a pearl, and a similar double meaning occurs in several European languages; in English, too, the daisy used to be called 'herb-margaret', 'meadow pearl' and, by Chaucer, who was very fond of daisies, 'douce Margarette'.

Marguerite or Margaret is also, of course, a woman's name and throughout history a large number of famous Margarets have assumed the flower as their emblem. Margaret of Anjou wore it as her device and had it embroidered on the sleeves of her courtiers and woven into chaplets to be entwined in their hair. Margaret, the sister of François I of France, also wore the daisy motif and was called by her brother 'Marguerite of Marguerites', pearl of pearls.

The marguerite or daisy was associated with several saints, most notably with St Margaret of Cortona who, after a mis-spent girlhood, repented and was canonized. However, because of her early adventures, she was invoked by young women suffering from uterine disorders and other complaints, including those of love requited and unrequited. An old ballad tells:

> *There is a double flowret, white and red,*
> *That our lasses call Herb Margaret,*
> *In honour of Cortona's penitent,*
> *Whose contrite soul with red remorse was rent:*
> *While on her penitence kind Heaven did throw*
> *The White of purity surpassing snow;*
> *So white and red in this fair flower entwine,*
> *Which maids are wont to scatter at her shrine.*

Marigold

CALENDULA (OR TAGETES)

Native:	Height:	Flowers:	Duration:
N. Hemisphere	8–24in.	May–October	about 4 months

To many English gardeners, the bright flare of the marigold has long been a way of bridging the gap between the riotous colours of spring and the muted hues of autumn; some marigold species, indeed, overcome all and continue well into the first frosts.

Marigolds, it seems, belong to everyone. In India, they decorate Hindu festivals; in Mexico they were said to spring from the blood of Aztecs who had died at the hands of the gold-hungry Conquistadores; the Romans called them *calendula* because in their gentle climate the flowers apparently blossomed the calendar round; and in Christian mythology generally it was held that marigolds were so named from the Virgin Mary who wore the blossoms in her bosom.

Sixteenth-century housewives used marigolds in salads and as a cheap and efficient substitute for saffron, and approved the inclusion of their petals in ointments for the complexion. In the same era, Shakespeare noted the flower's habit of closing at dusk and opening with the morning dew: 'The marigold that goes to bed with the sun, and with him rises weeping'. But perhaps his loveliest hymn to the morning comes from *Cymbeline*:

> *Hark! Hark! the lark at heaven's gate sings*
> *And Phoebus 'gins arise*
> *His steeds to water at those springs*
> *On chalic'd flowers that lies;*
> *And winking Mary-buds begin*
> *To ope their golden eyes . . .*

Mary-buds are, of course, marigolds.

Michaelmas daisy

⁂ ASTER NOVAE-ANGLIAE ⁂

Native:	Height:	Flowers:	Duration:
N. America	4–5 ft.	September–October	4–5 weeks

None of the dozen or so species of garden plants that we think of as Michaelmas daisies— *Aster novi-belgii, A. novae-angliae* and the rest—is native to Britain. They are all fairly recent importations, mostly from North America. Though some may be seen making a brave show along railway cuttings and on waste ground, bending beneath the autumn winds, these are simply refugees from domesticity exhibiting a magnificent ability to adapt.

Only one plant of the salt marshes, and one seldom seen, is truly entitled to be called Michaelmas daisy, because it is sacred to St Michael the Archangel. It always blooms on or about his day, 29 September; but then so do the others, and even if they have assumed his name more recently, probably Michael—soldier, patron of boats and horsemen—would not mind. Michaelmas has always been a day of colour and pageantry, of great end-of-harvest fairs in England, and of horse-racing and feasting upon special cakes in the north of Scotland.

Though they have but lately crossed the Atlantic, Michaelmas daisies are nevertheless closely related to the asters of the Old World, or the 'star-worts', as the English used to call them. The purple-blue *Aster amellus*, the Italian starwort, has been identified as the flower that was woven into wreaths and strewn on the altars of the Greek gods, while throughout northern Europe girls plucked petals from several different kinds of asters in the age-old game 'He loves me; he loves me not'.

Mint

(APPLEMINT, OR SPEAR/GARDEN MINT)
MENTHA ROTUNDIFLORA (OR M. SPICATA)

Native:	Height:	Flowers:	Duration:
Europe, N. Asia	24in.	July–September	6 weeks

As long ago as 1398, an English gardener ruefully noted that 'Mynte of gardens is an herbe that multiplyeth itselfe', showing that even then, when much greater use was made of the various mints than is the case today, it was still possible to have too much of a good thing. There are literally dozens of species of mint, all prolific and all with a number of uses, though in our own time we tend to ignore most of them and concentrate upon only a few. Authorities differ as to whether apple or garden mint is best for cooking, but both are widely employed, and peppermint provides us with menthol for all kinds of medicines and lotions. Without these mints society would be bereft of *crème de menthe*, Chartreuse, Benedictine and much of its chewing gum, but sadly, no one now seems to bother about hairy, water, bergamot, downy, curly or horse mints. Even pennyroyal, which was carried in great quantities on board ships to sweeten fouled water casks, is largely forgotten.

Like so many other herbs, mint is said to have been brought to Britain by the Romans. Pliny observed that the smell of mint 'doth stir up the mind and taste to a greedy desire of meat', so it is not surprising that mint sauce has had its place on good tables since at least the third century AD. An even shrewder innovation was the inclusion of mint in tooth-cleaning preparations; this seems to have been first suggested in the sixth century.

Gerard says that the herb is an excellent defence against 'Beare-wormes, Sea-scorpions and Serpents', but it was perhaps more widely used to rid kennels and clothes-chests of fleas and moths.

MENTHA ROTUNDIFLORA

MENTHA SPICATA

Nasturtium

⟶ ː TROPAEOLUM MAJUS ː ⟵

Native:	Height	Flowers:	Duration:
S. America	8ft.	June–September	6–8 weeks

The flowers are radiant, vital, cheerfully tropical and, like the leaves, edible—all of which are excellent reasons for nasturtiums to have been planted in such abundance upon Anderson air-raid shelters in London back gardens during the Second World War.

The plant was brought from the West Indies to Europe in 1574, and reached England some time in the 1590s. The problem was, what should it be called? Its hot, peppery flavour, akin to that of watercress, was noted, and so for a time it was known as Indian cresses. It would have been better if it had remained that way, for when generic names were awarded to plants, watercress was labelled as being of the genus *Nasturtium*, meaning, roughly, 'nose-twister', a reminder of its pepperiness. Somehow, this became the common name of the plant from the Indies, which is no relation at all. So, perhaps to make amends, it was given a much more poetic name of its own; *Tropaeolum* means 'trophy', a reference to its shield-shaped leaves and flowers like golden helmets, which together resemble some ancient trophy of war.

When Gerard completed his *Herball* in 1597, Indian cresses were practically stop-press news, so he can be forgiven for saying that 'We have no certaine knowledge of his nature and vertues' and for referring the case 'to later consideration'. Fortunately, later generations have completed his work, and now nasturtium leaves and flowers are chopped into salads, sandwich fillings and cream cheese. The seeds can also be used in pickles as a substitute for capers.

Opium poppy

——:PAPAVER SOMNIFERUM:——

Native:	Height	Flowers:	Duration:
Asia, Europe	2½ft.	June–August	about 10 days

O nce upon a time, a mouse shared a hut on the banks of the Ganges with a wise man. They were very fond of each other, but the mouse was discontented with her lot, and asked to be transformed into a cat. The wise man obliged, but she liked being a cat no better, and so in rapid succession was transformed into a dog, a boar, an elephant and, finally, a beautiful maiden. One day, a king chanced by the hut. On seeing the girl, he fell deeply in love with her and insisted that she and the wise man should at once come to live with him in his palace. They were all very happy until the girl missed her footing in the garden, fell down a well and was drowned. The king was inconsolable, but the wise man comforted him, saying, 'We shall bury her where she lies, and from her bones a flower will spring, which we shall call the poppy. And whoever partakes of the juice of the poppy will remember her, for he will be mischievous as a mouse, fond of milk as a cat, noisy as a dog, savage as a boar, lumbering as an elephant and— arrogant as a queen.'

It does not seem that opium was used as a narcotic much before the seventeenth century, when the habit of smoking it gradually spread from China. But as a drug for relieving the pains of cholera, dysentery and childbirth, it has been known for at least two thousand years. It was always obtained in the same way, by tapping the white juice from the seed-pod within three weeks of the poppy's flowering, and drying it, which also gives us morphine and codeine.

The seeds themselves contain no drug, and were widely used as a spice in the Middle Ages; they are still used, scattered over various breads and cakes.

Pansy

⸺ ⫶VIOLA TRICOLOR⫶ ⸺

Native:	Height:	Flowers:	Duration:
Europe	2–6in.	May–September	2–3 months

Ophelia provides a clue to the origin of the most usual name for this charming flower when she gives some to her brother and says, 'There's Pansies; that's for thoughts'—the name is derived from the French *pensée*, a thought, and the flower has long been said to symbolize the mental processes of lovers.

Perhaps this was what Oberon had in mind when, in *A Midsummer Night's Dream*, he despatched Puck to fetch him 'love-in-idleness'—an old country name for the pansy—whose juice,

> *. . . on sleeping eyelids laid,*
> *Will make man or woman madly dote*
> *Upon the first live creature that it sees.*

He squeezed the juice upon the eyelids of Titania, who, on waking, fell passionately in love with the donkey-headed Bottom.

That the flower can also bring comfort to lovers is apparent in a third name, 'heart's-ease', which originated long ago when a number of maidens died of love, or, as Robert Herrick put it in the seventeenth century,

> *Ran for sweethearts mad and died.*
> *Love, in pity of their tears*
> *And their loss in blooming years,*
> *For their restless here-spent hours,*
> *Gave them Heart's-ease turned to flowers.*

Peony
⸺⁚PAEONIA OFFICINALIS⁚⸺

Native:	Height:	Flowers:	Duration:
S. Europe	2ft.	May–June	about 4 weeks

The peony was held to be one of those plants which, like the mandrake, is uprooted by men only at their peril, since its screams during the process will kill anyone within earshot. The only way to transplant it, therefore, was to tie a hungry dog to its base, and place a piece of meat a little out of reach so that, in endeavouring to acquire the meat, the dog would haul the peony out of the ground. One would think that experiment would have shown the fallacy of this, but perhaps in ancient times no one ever dared to attempt the uprooting of the plant in any other way. Could it be that some long-ago gardener, noticing how much peonies detest being moved, invented this lurid tale to protect them? Certainly, peonies left undisturbed will bloom quite happily in the same situation for fifty years or more.

Country people—those who dared to dig them up—used to carve peony roots into necklaces as a charm against all kinds of maladies, presumably because of the plant's association with Paeon, physician to the Greek gods. It could also be drunk in black-cherry water, and a peony-red complexion was held to be a sign of good health. Other authorities disagree, and say that the flower's colour is a blush of guilt, since once it was a shepherdess who yielded to the advances of the sun god. But apparently she was forgiven, since,

> *'Twas Phoebus' crime, who in his arms allured*
> *A maid from all mankind by pride assured.*

Periwinkle

⸭VINCA MAJOR⸭

Native: Europe	Height: 6–12in.	Flowers: April–June, occasionally also September–October	Duration: 6 weeks

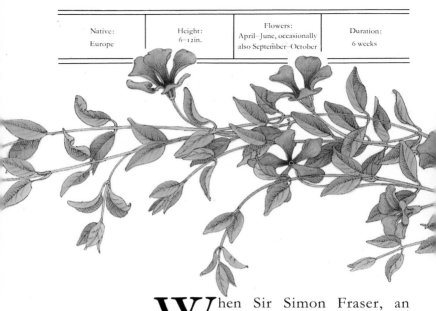

When Sir Simon Fraser, an adherent of the Scottish patriot Sir William Wallace, was led out to execution in 1306, a bystander noted: 'Y-fetered were ys legges under his horse's wombe ... a garland of perewenke set on ys head', and throughout the Middle Ages to say that someone was crowned with periwinkle meant that he was destined for the gallows.

Why this modest and charming little flower should have been selected for so macabre a role is uncertain. Both the Italian and Spanish names for it mean 'flower of death', but in these countries it had nothing to do with executions; rather, it was twined about the bodies of dead children and planted on their graves.

On a more cheerful note, the plant was also regarded as being sacred to Venus, which probably led to Culpeper the herbalist's statement that if it were eaten in a salad by a man and wife, it would provoke love between them, 'which is a rare qualitie if true', he added doubtfully.

Pink

:DIANTHUS:

Native:	Height:	Flowers:	Duration:
N. Hemisphere	10—12in.	June	3–4 weeks

It has long been the charming practice of our native poets, when evoking images of the countryside, to recite long lists of the delightful common names of British flowers. Take Edmund Spenser, for example, in his *Shepheard's Calendar*:

> *Bring hither the Pink and purple Columbine*
> *With Gillyflowers*
> *Bring Coronation, and Sops in wine*
> *Worn of paramours . . .*

The trouble is that though he and his near-contemporaries know what these terms meant, they are a little imprecise for us. Pink, coronation (carnation) and gillyflowers are all species of *Dianthus*, except that sometimes 'gillyflower' meant 'pink', and sometimes referred to the unrelated wallflower. Often, too, the flowers have changed in appearance since their day, so that when Pepys noted that he went 'to the old Spring Garden, where the wenches gathered pinks', or Gerard observed that 'a wild, creeping pink groweth in our pastures ... but especially in the great field next to Detford', we cannot be certain that they saw the same pinks as we know today. There is a Deptford pink still, but there are also Indian, Chinese, clove, Spanish, swamp, wild and many other kinds of pinks beside. It is all rather confusing. But whatever flower they did mean was said to have got its name from *Pinkster*, a Dutch word for Whitsun, since one species bloomed at that time.

It was believed that to drink vinegar in which pinks had been steeped was efficacious against the plague.

Primrose

——:PRIMULA VULGARIS:——

Native:	Height:	Flowers:	Duration:
UK	6in.	March–April	3–5 weeks

When Benjamin Disraeli, Lord Beaconsfield, was dying, it is said that Queen Victoria sent him a bunch of primroses, picked by her own hand, and with them a note that read: 'They were *his* favourite flower', referring to Albert, her beloved Prince Consort, who had died some twenty years earlier. Disraeli smiled wanly. 'I hope,' he said, 'that Her Majesty does not mean me to deliver them in person.'

Out of this, or out of other versions of the story, there arose the idea that primroses were Disraeli's favourite flower (though there is no confirmation that he ever expressed any opinion about them), and so the Primrose League, dedicated to his ideals, was born. And 19 April, the anniversary of his death, was set apart by the League to be celebrated as Primrose Day in perpetuity.

Probably Disraeli did not know, and if he did he would not have cared, that in many parts of Britain it was long believed that to bring a single primrose into the house was a certain omen of a death in the family; in other areas, it was considered that to gather less than thirteen primroses at a time was a danger to livestock. In the West Country too, it was said that you should never take less than a handful of primroses into a farmhouse; to ignore this rule would be to endanger the ducklings. On the other hand, the primrose was held to be one of the flowers that bloomed in Paradise, and to those who were lucky enough to pick an earthly one with six leaves it would be of enormous benefit in affairs of the heart. As John Donne put it,

The primrose, when with six leaves gotten grace
Maids, as a true love, in their bosoms place.

Rose

—:(WHITE ROSE OF YORK) ROSA × ALBA:——

Native:	Height:	Flowers:	Duration:
Europe	6ft. plus	June	3–4 weeks

There are roses of Tralee, of Picardy and of No Man's Land, but in British lore and legend, as cricketers, historians and others are aware, there are few flowers of greater significance than the so-called White Rose of York. It is probably a hybrid of extremely ancient origin, so ancient that Pliny in his day suggested that Britain's old name of Albion was derived not from her white cliffs but from her white roses. The flower's association with Yorkshire began in the mid-fifteenth century in the Temple Gardens, according to tradition and Shakespeare, when the rival Houses of York and Lancaster chose a white and a red rose as their respective emblems in battle. *Rose × alba* is generally said to be the Yorkist rose and *Rosa gallica officinalis* the one selected by the Lancastrians. But there is another rose, of uncertain variety, associated with the Wars of the Roses; this is the mysterious flower that is still believed to bloom on the battlefield of Towton in Yorkshire, where both sides suffered severe casualties. Apparently it will grow nowhere else.

James II had been Duke of York before his accession, so that after his exile his white rose emblem became that of the Jacobite cause—the White Cockade, 'the Rose that's like the snow'. As such it figures in many of the ballads of the Jacobite Rebellions, and of their tragic aftermaths:

> *My father's blude's in that fluir-tap,*
> *My brither's in that hare-bell's blossom,*
> *This White Rose was steeped in my luve's blude,*
> *An' aye I'll wear it in my bosom.*

Rosemary

ROSMARINUS OFFICINALIS

Native: Mediterranean	Height: to 6ft.	Flowers: April–September	Duration: 3 months plus

No old-time herbalist would have considered his stock complete without rosemary, and even modern ones prescribe it to aid digestion, to improve circulation, and as a hair rinse. And, of course, it is excellent with roast lamb. However, this list is negligible compared with that of a few centuries ago when the plant was used to drive away moths, restore fading eyesight, improve hearing, cure all manner of diseases and clear the skin, or with Gerard, as a remedy against 'stuffing of the head and a cold braine'. Most wonderful, according to Parkinson in 1640, was an oil made of the flowers, which had to be put into a bottle and then 'digested in hot horse dung' for two weeks.

But its best-known use was as an aid to memory, whence came its even more famous role as a symbol of remembrance. Lovers and old friends would present sprigs of rosemary, as Ophelia did in *Hamlet*, and it was often strewn on graves. St Thomas More said it was 'sacred to remembrance, and therefore to friendship . . . a sprig hath a dumb language that maketh it the chosen emblem at our funeral wakes and in our burial grounds'; and in some parts of the country bunches of rosemary may still be laid on coffin lids.

Most poignant was its appearance at the funerals of young girls, where the themes of death and lost love mingled—themes that particularly appealed to poets. Thus Robert Southey, in his *Bride's Burial*:

> *When villagers my shroud bestrew*
> *With pansies, rosemary and rue,*
> *Then, Lady, weave a wreath for me,*
> *But weave it of the cypress tree.*

Rue

─────: RUTA GRAVEOLENS :─────

Native:	Height:	Flowers:	Duration:
Europe	2–5 ft.	June–August	3–4 weeks

In one of his livelier works, A.E. Housman describes how, not so very long ago, it was the custom to bury suicides at crossroads, giving this as the reason why 'sinner's rue' so often grows in such places. Chancing by a crossroads grave, the poet picks the flowers because,

> *It seemed a herb of healing,*
> *A balsam and a sign,*
> *Flower of a heart whose trouble*
> *Must have been worse than mine.*

Whether rue grows any more readily at crossroads than anywhere else is uncertain, but there is no doubt that the herb's association with sorrow and repentance goes back a long way. Several reasons are suggested. It may be due to a confusion of the name with 'ruth', an old word for pity or remorse; it may be that water of rue was sprinkled by the priest upon his congregation in pre-Reformation days; or perhaps it was simply that the bitter taste of the leaves is akin to that of repentance.

For many years, the herb figured in pious puns. 'Rue in thyme should be a maiden's posy' is fairly typical. Then, in the late eighteenth century, the connection with repentance was confirmed. At that time, epidemics of gaol fever—typhus—swept through Newgate and other British prisons, and, in the belief that pungent rue was a disinfectant, sheaves of it were spread on the floors of cells and courtrooms. A bunch is still laid before judges at assizes, though whether as a defence against contagion or as a hint that remorse might be rewarded with mercy is forgotten.

92

Sage

—:SALVIA OFFICINALIS:—

Native:	Height:	Flowers:	Duration:
S. Europe	2ft.	June–July	about 2 weeks

It seems odd, but the marriage between sage and onion was not announced until Mrs Hannah Glasse produced her classic *Art of Cookery* in 1747. Yet whispers of the courtship had been going on for a long time, to judge by *Haven Health*, published in 1594, which says that the herb 'is used commonly in sawces as to stuffe veale, porke, rosting pigges ... and that for good cawse', the author adds enthusiastically.

But millennia before the plant's culinary advantages were noted the ancients were aware of its medicinal properties—which is why they called it *salvia*, from the Latin *salvare*, to save or cure. They ascribed to it all kinds of virtues: the ability to cure ague and fever, especially if eaten, as they used to say in Sussex, 'nine days fasting', and to promote longevity. The perseverance of the last notion is apparent in the old English saw:

> *He that would live for aye,*
> *Must eat Sage in May.*

Why May is specified is not clear, but tradition firmly maintains that to eat sage with butter and parsley in that month is very good for you. An infusion of sage leaves will serve either as a mouthwash or as a hair conditioner; and perhaps we should also bear in mind the seventeenth-century adage:

> *These for frenzy be*
> *A speedy and a sovereigne remedy;*
> *The bitter wormwood, sage and marigold.*

Altogether a very obliging plant, it seems.

Snowdrop

⸭GALANTHUS NIVALIS⸭

Native:	Height:	Flowers:	Duration:
Europe	3–8in.	December onwards	2–3 weeks

This lovely little plant, whether coddled in a greenhouse or grown outdoors, seems to gear its appearance to the first thaw, whenever it may occur. Even so, an old English tradition insists:

The Snowdrop, in purest white arraie,
First rears her hedde on Candlemass Day,

though in the milder parts of the country it usually blooms well before this date, 2 February. But as in any account of this harbinger of spring, the accent is on the snowdrop's purity. At one time, on the Feast of the Purification, on Candlemas Day, it was the custom that maidens, dressed in white, should carry snowdrops to church and strew them on the altar. Hence the plant's old name of 'maid of February'; it was sacred to virgins and in consequence was often planted in convent gardens.

There is a legend that tells how a passing angel, hearing Eve weeping in a wintry Eden, when no flowers grew, seized a snowflake and breathed upon it, so turning it into a snowdrop. He gave it to Eve, and said:

This is an earnest, Eve, to thee,
That sun and summer soon shall be.

Where the angel stood, a ring of snowdrops grew, and Eve was said to have cherished them more than any other flowers in Eden. Another old story, however, says that they were born one spring when the Virgin set out across the hills to visit St Elizabeth; and that, wherever her foot touched, snowdrops grew.

Solomon's seal

POLYGONATUM MULTIFLORUM

Native:	Height:	Flowers:	Duration:
Europe	2–4ft.	June	1 month

If the thick, knobbly root of this plant is cut across, it leaves a scar which might be translated as the five-pointed seal of Solomon, source of inspiration and power, and passport to the Kingdom of Light. However, Gerard, in his *Herball* of 1597, is more inclined to ascribe the name to the root's wonderful ability to seal any wound it is laid upon and to take away, overnight, 'any blacke or blew spots gotten by womens wilfulnesse, in stumbling upon their hasty husband's fists, or such like'. In his day too, 'the vulgar sort of people in Hampshire' used to pound the roots, mix the juice with a little ale, and swallow the draught as a cure for broken bones, or internal bruising or bleeding. Equally, the mixture could be applied as a poultice to limbs that were out of joint, swollen or inflamed, with swift and beneficial results.

Stonecrops

──:(BITING STONECROP) SEDUM ACRE :──

Native:	Height:	Flowers:	Duration:
Europe	1–2in.	June–July	3–4 weeks

One of the most endearing alternative names for biting stonecrop was 'Welcome-home-husband-though-never-so-drunk'; apparently a liquor made by boiling the leaves in water was used as an emetic for those who had imbibed too freely. It was also known as 'pricke-madame', 'mousetail', 'wall-pepper', 'country-pepper' and 'Jack-of-the-buttery'.

The plant is a succulent, with water-storing tissue in its leaves, and is therefore well adapted to growing on walls; one of the summer delights of the Cotswolds is to see the plant tumbling in great starry masses over the warm stone.

Sedums of many different varieties have long been grown in British gardens; a particular old-time favourite was the red-flowering orpine (*S. telephium*), also known as 'live-long', 'midsummer-men', 'harping-johnnie' and 'live-long-love-long', the last name arising from the plant's use in love spells. At one time, particularly in the West Country, it was the custom for young girls to gather the plant at midsummer and hang it up in their bedrooms. If by the next morning the flowers had turned to the right, then their lovers would remain true to them; if to the left, they would be unfaithful. The eighteenth-century poet Hannah More says:

> *Now once a year, so country records tell,*
> *When o'er the heath sounds out the midnight bell,*
> *The Eve of Midsummer, that foe to sleep,*
> *What time young maids their annual vigil keep,*
> *The tell-tale shrub fresh gathered to declare*
> *The swains who're false from those that faithful are.*

Sunflower
:HELIANTHUS ANNUS:

Native:	Height:	Flowers:	Duration:
S. America	3–10ft.	July–September	3–4 weeks

Sunflowers, big and yellow as brass warming-pans, still have an exotic air in English gardens, though they have been popular here ever since they were first introduced from the Americas in the days of Queen Elizabeth I; and it cannot be denied that a clump of them, nodding their tall heads at the back of a wide border, adds just the right touch of garishness to the end of the summer.

The notion that they keep their faces turned always to the sun has been a long time a-dying, chiefly because the image was so pleasing to poets. As Blake says:

> *Ah, Sunflower! weary of time,*
> *Who countest the steps of the sun,*
> *Seeking after that sweet golden clime,*
> *Where the traveller's journey is done.*

And Thomas Moore:

> *As the sunflower turns on her god, when he sets,*
> *The same look which she turn'd when he rose.*

In fact, it does nothing of the kind, and the flower's name is really derived from its being sacred to the sun god of the Incas of Peru, since it so resembled the sun. According to the Conquistadores, the Inca priestesses were crowned with carved sunflowers of pure gold, and the temples were decorated in the same way.

Sunflower oil, extracted from the crushed seeds, is excellent for cooking, and Gerard, who would try anything once, says that the buds, boiled and eaten with butter and vinegar are 'exceeding pleasant meat'.

Sweet-william

⁚DIANTHUS BARBATUS⁚

Native:	Height:	Flowers:	Duration:
E. Europe	12–24in.	June–July	4–5 weeks

There is a legend in Scotland that this flower is named after William Augustus, Duke of Cumberland, the portly third son of George II and victor of Culloden. He is better known to history as 'Butcher' Cumberland for the atrocities he committed upon the Jacobite wounded after the battle; but, in 1746, so grateful was London for deliverance from the threat of the northern barbaric hordes that bonfires were lit in the streets and the hero's path was strewn with petals. Handel composed an oratorio in his honour, inns were rechristened 'The Duke's Head', Tyburn Gate into Hyde Park, beside the famous gallows, was rather appropriately renamed Cumberland Gate, and a flower was given the name of 'sweet william'. In dour retaliation, the Jacobites christened the evil-smelling common ragwort 'Stinking Billy'.

In fact, sweet-william was so called long before Cumberland's day, and may well have been originally named after St William of Rochester, since the flowers grew in profusion in that part of Kent. As long ago as the 1590s they were 'esteemed for their beauty to decke up gardens, the bosomes of the beautifull, garlands and crownes for pleasure', and for centuries have been a part of the English summer's pageant. Matthew Arnold chides a friend bent on foreign travel:

> *Too quick despairer, wherefore wilt thou go?*
> *Soon will the high Midsummer pomps come on,*
> *Soon will the musk carnations break and swell,*
> *Soon shall we have gold-dusted snapdragon,*
> *Sweet-william with his homely cottage smell*
> *And stocks in fragrant blow . . .*

Valerian

——: VALERIANA OFFICINALIS :——

Native:	Height:	Flowers:	Duration:
Europe, N. Asia	3–5 ft.	June–August	7–10 days

As anyone knows who has ever damaged a root of it in the garden, valerian puts forth a most curious odour, repulsive and fetid to the modern nostril. Cats love it, however, and if faced with it will go into a kind of ecstasy, tearing the plant to pieces, eating the roots and purring like dynamos. Topsell, in his *Four-footed Beastes* (1681), says: 'The root of the herb valerian (commonly called Phu) is very like the eye of a cat, and wheresoever it groweth, if cats come thereunto, they instantly dig it up for the love thereof ... for it smelleth moreover like a cat'. Rats, too, adore it; old-time ratcatchers used to bait their traps with it, and it is said that the secret of the Pied Piper's success was that his pockets were filled with valerian roots. His music was only incidental.

But it seems that man did not always regard the odour as unpleasant. The perfume spikenard, often mentioned in the Bible, was made from valerian, the Romans used it as incense, and both Arabs and mediaeval Europeans regarded it as an aphrodisiac.

The name means, roughly, to fare well, or be healthy, and the importance of valerian as a medicinal herb was noted as long ago as the fifth century BC. It was grown in monastery gardens and figures prominently in Anglo-Saxon herbal remedies of the eleventh century.

Even modern herbalists say that it is the best of all herbal tranquillizers. A teaspoonful of the roots soaked for twelve hours in water and the infusion drunk one hour before bed for several nights running will ensure a sweet sleep. But it should not be persevered with for too long, or lethargy and headaches will ensue.

Violet

——: VIOLA ODORATA :——

Native:	Height:	Flowers:	Duration:
Europe, Asia, N. Africa	4–6in.	February–April	2–3 weeks

Bards from Homer to Al Jolson have sung the joys of this enchanting flower, but have dressed it in such simile, metaphor and symbolism as to be bewildering. The tales of its origin are many, and seem to be equally divided between the flower's scent and its colour. One version says that when Zeus transformed Io (Greek: *Ion*, violet) into a white heifer, her breath was so sweet that violets grew wherever she breathed, while another claims that they are maidens beaten blue by Venus for envy of their beauty.

To most of us, violets represent everything that is youthful and spring-like, but to Shakespeare there was something wistful about them, and it is in this mood that they appear in *Hamlet*. Laertes speaks of 'A violet in the youth of primy nature, Forward, not permanent, sweet, not lasting'; Ophelia would have given violets but 'they withered all when my father died'; and Laertes again, at his sister's graveside, prays that 'from her fair and unpolluted flesh, may violets spring'.

Violets were often a symbol of death, and were carried at funerals. But they also signified constancy and faithfulness, which was why they were adopted as the badge of the exiled Emperor Napoleon, 'the flower that returns in the spring'. Byron has Bonaparte declaiming, on his departure for Elba,

> *Farewell to thee, France! but when liberty rallies*
> *Once more in thy regions, remember me then;*
> *The Violet grows in the depths of thy valleys,*
> *Though withered, thy tears will unfold it again.*

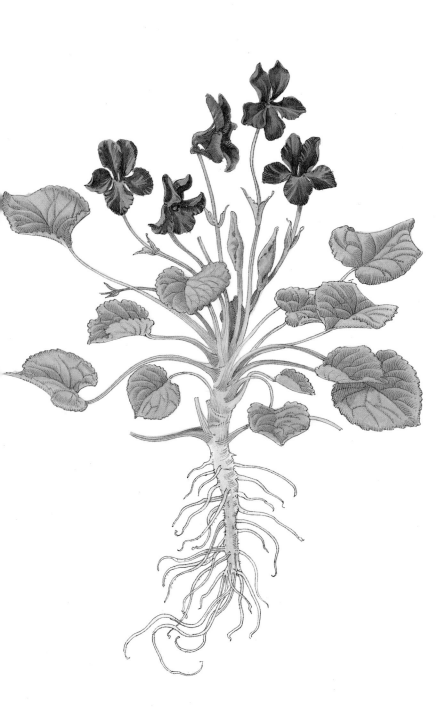

Wallflower
——:CHEIRANTHUS CHEIRI:——

Native:	Height:	Flowers:	Duration:
Europe	to 18in.	April–June	6 weeks

The plant shares the old name of 'gillyflower' with pinks and carnations, thus giving rise to a certain amount of confusion. In fact, it is a member of the stock family, and when it was introduced from Spain many centuries ago it was known as 'stock-gillofer'; later, when its habit of inserting itself in the cracks of old walls was noted, it was called 'wall-gillyflower'. Perhaps it was this same habit that made the plant a favourite with troubadours who were given to singing of their love outside castle walls and, since wallflowers were the blooms most ready to hand, they made bouquets of them and wore or presented them as a symbol of undying adoration. The plant was believed to prevent ulcers.

The appellation of 'wallflower' to a girl who does not choose to dance, or who is not asked, and therefore sits by the wall, goes back to 1820 at least; but according to legend, the name had a rather more complimentary beginning. It seems that a young Border laird fell in love with the daughter of a rival family and, after several unsuccessful attempts at elopement, persuaded her to climb out of a window in her father's castle. Robert Herrick takes up the tale:

> *Up she got upon a wall,*
> *Attempted down to slide withal.*
> *But the silken twist untied*
> *So she fell and bruised, died.*
> *Love in pity of the deed,*
> *And her loving luckless speed,*
> *Turn'd her to this plant we call*
> *Now the Flower of the Wall.*

Select Bibliography

Among the many authorities consulted during the preparation of this book, the author is particularly grateful to the following:

Mrs Beeton   *Household Management*
Rupert Brooke   *1914 and Other Poems*
Geoffrey Chaucer   *Canterbury Tales*
Nicholas Culpeper   *British Herbal*
Michael Drayton   *Collected Works*
Rev. H. Friend   *Flowers and Flower Lore*
R. Folkard   *Plant lore, legend and lyrics*
John Gerard   *Herball*
John Keats   *Collected Works*
John Last   *The Herb Book*
Pliny   *Natural History*
Sir Walter Scott   *Border Ballads*
William Shakespeare   *Collected Works*
W. Turner   *The Herball*
Thomas Tusser   *500 Points of Husbandry*
Tynan & Maitland   *The Book of Flowers*